How to Not Write a Sonnet

Aedan Cowell

BookLeaf Publishing

India | USA | UK

Presentation by *BookLeaf Publishing*

Web: www.bookleafpub.com

E-mail: info@bookleafpub.com

ISBN: 9789357449397

First edition 2022

DEDICATION

Dedicated to my late grandfather, Laurie, who passed a few days before I began this project. He was a beacon of joy to those around him, an outspoken man of God, and an inspiration to so many, myself included.

ACKNOWLEDGEMENT

I want to acknowledge the major part played by my friend, Hayley, who told me about this publishing opportunity and regularly went out of their way to encourage me regarding my writing. I want to also acknowledge my family, as they always encouraged me to write and share my work, even when I avoided doing either for so long.
Finally, I want to acknowledge my God, who acts as my original and ultimate inspiration.

PREFACE

This collection of poetry is the culmination of a few years of sporadic periods of writing. It wasn't until I began to collate the works I felt were most complete that I realised they were all intrinsically connected. This was not purposeful on my part. Or maybe it was. I'm still not fully sure.

Themes vary throughout this collection, but the primary focus revolves around how good we are at lying to and blinding ourselves, while subconsciously projecting our falsehoods onto those around us.

Aurora's Reprise

Thin, dark fingers draw back that black curtain
as turquoise hues usher forth uncertain
and naïve hope. She makes no foolish vow,
offers no consolatory pledge. Sow
beaming seeds beautiful as you carry
your terrible noose and paint starry
canvas blue. Your golden apple rises
and carelessly lights blood red horizons,
killing my tranquil rest. A distant clock
does tick, tick, tick past half past six as
cockcrow
mocks my slow rise and groggy eyes. I wish
those
hands would stop turning, ticking, tugging claws
that carve deep scars and leave the heart
yearning.
The Dawn brings only sadness and morning.

Careless Storytelling

I still joyfully reap torment, slaving
away to feel that same pain I've felt one
thousand times. Finally able, braving
these bastard feelings I thought might be gone,
I continue to write our shared chapter
that we place in different books. Each touch
reads different, every look tortures
the same, and each whisper still means too
much.
A wisp at fog-cursed dusk, you slip away
even as I cling to ethereal
hope that, someday soon, you might choose to
stay
and watch the sun die its death so cruel.
Such a fool, into your arms I hurry,
and carelessly tell my awful story.

Loss?

A seat above the clouds
before the transcendent view,
I touch the sky but feel
lonely without you.

But this perch, up in
high mountain cleft,
is only possible
because you left.

Internal Bleeding

Held hostage by platonic affection,
I prithy be lover's touch. The yearning
cuts so deep you see my sinews flare. Thin
skin sun-blistered and uninteresting.
Take your leave that I might breathe for a while
and gasp in the biting dusk, drowned under
intentions once pure but since sent senile.
Shallow waters disturbed by ceased slumber,
stirred and frothing but silent and wily,
your heart's tossing then falls still suddenly.

Breathless

I shan't obsess over your loyalty,
for why would the affections in you be
loyal to me. Though this interest be wild
and my dreams be wistful, this love be mild
but be love in full. Oh, but it can't be.
Will love, so aloof, stoop to humour me?
But no. You are the beauty to my beast
You are the Fanny to my sickly Keats
Move, breathe, be entirely the you
that brings me to my reverent knee, due
for fervent plea. So shallow is thee
that I know. More lies where my eyes can't see.
Vast, unexplored depths hide so far beneath
your mask. Sagacity stays in willing sheathe,
and festers in that ever-restless sleep.
Oh, do I truly expect what lay deep
within your sea? How might I question this?
Beauty be bliss when the inward's amiss
When spirits yearn for mere youthful degree
is when wiser fellows, like swift deer, flee.
But can I fly from the nest that I do
not know? Escape from places I wish go?
Rage heaven, answer your now lost son
and give me reason. I have not yet run
as younger love have I, like fool, harboured
and for long'r ages have I not laboured?
Why, for far lesser love did I not suffer?

Doth cruel time threaten to passion wither?
I might discern my portion is not her.
I know greater love, and even grander
love than that. Love that conquers great distress!
Yet I know of love worth immensely less
that men have bled and given 'way life for.
Hear my humble plea, is there truly more?

Merciless Tides

Driftwood cast down cruel sea, rotten
and cracked. We tire of grasping for
breathe. Passing many a sunken
vessel, dismissed by those that still
float. Cursed, alone, and crumbling.
Then comes that portentous moment,
face-to-face with that essence which
frames the awful, salt-ridden bones
of your own being. A brief reprieve
shared but forgotten as we both
drift away on merciless tides.

Darling Child

Your love is the ethereal wind in my sails,
ushering me to depart for foreign aisles.
The great power that drives me forth calls your
lovely
heart home, and beckons me to unknowable sea.
Unfeasible, it pushes me to thoughtless deed,
Mysterious, it draws me in to lovely creed.
My reasons to live are but few, but my foremost
reason is you. My heart wish be your loves sole
host.
Like spring bloom, my soul bursts forth at your
season,
you liberate the shackled, this life my prison.
There are none that drive my mind to cravings
so deep,
and that guide my obsessions, like shepherd to
sheep.
Do I truly know you? The depths of your soul
escape
my fickle mind. You're too distant, your words
create
passion and confusion as I grasp to see the
lowest of your qualities. You love me,
I know, but you're love for me I cannot.
Carry me, lift me to that great thought
that I might begin to grasp the grandeur
of your great affection for me. Hearts stir

at the whisper of your call and at the
boom of your voice they can't but plea, "mercy!"
Yet you have gifted forgiveness to slaves,
liberation offered love to craven
scum and thieves, making this dark heart sing
wild.
Cradle me in your arms, your darling child.

Victimised and Validated

I am nothing. A cockroach
under your heel. A disease
you thought was a reproach
for you to purge. With ease
you laid a trap for me and
hid to watch me fall into
it and suffer. You call, I stand
to answer. Thinking I know
you, I gorge myself on
your poison until I am
ill and that sickness
makes me feel
valid.

It makes me feel how you
never could. It's tough
to be a bug.

Hidden from Me

I heard
from a friend

that your mind
doesn't shout and
knock things about

that you can be
alone without
memory's haunt

that when you lay down
and shut your eyes
that the world goes quiet

and you sleep

and

I need to know
where you found
that silence?

Better Left Unsaid

Buzzing phone left dormant on
wooden bedside table. Caller's
ID, so undesired. Long gone
are the days of hearing that
chatter, of kind banter and
longing whisper. Unrequited
love left lying dormant,
a careless buzz does reignite it.
Festering wound weeps anew
as dormant affection, once unseen,
now renewed. I rise and reach to
pen a thought, obscene.
To write in loving memory
of that which could have been.

It's Never Anyone

It had been so long since you kissed
lips that whispered love and shared pain.
Suddenly, you see what you've missed,
why each past flame had been undone.

Staring into her caring eyes
you feel everything once again
and, finally, you realise,
that you could love anyone.

A Test

Yes, the weather *is* nice. It *has* been quite
warm. It *is* getting colder, you *are* right
about that. Um, no, nothing new with me.
Oh, no big deal, I just called to ask you
what your deepest and darkest fears might be?

Oh, just asking for a friend.

Flickering Light

The natural light
of my bedroom window
flickered from flight
of a passing sparrow.

A flicker again as
an eagle did follow
and the small bird was
consumed, bone and marrow.

Cruel chill crept close
across my pale face
as the Reaper's repose
did my room grace.

Thus, today was not the day
and this was not my time
but come tomorrow it may
occur that I reach the end of the line.

Homely Joys

In isolation, beauty resides in the mundane,
breath-taking hides in the home.
The day, a lovely game to seek and find the sane
that mischievously hides under your nose.
It fills the gaps in the refrigerator's whir,
that fragrance as the curry stir,
it's the affection hid
in lover's smile,
a message from a friend
not heard from in a while.
In dog's wagging tail
and piled-up junk mail.
In reading's transcendence
and blooming succulents.
It hides in subtle hue,
in the static crackle
of beloved chatter.
The beautiful lives alongside you,
so don't succumb to needless shackle,
reach out and hold her near.

Sand run coarse 'cross skin.
You focus on the texture,
and feel, for a time,

-Stranded.

Concrete Temples

You erect skyscrapers in reverence
of achievement and grasp for great grey clouds
in vanity, living life in severance
from your soul. You think your purpose is found
in gold, in vain deed, on these asphalt streets.
This your concrete temple hosts worship cruel
and liturgy unjust. Your stronghold bleak
but sturdy for the moment. Like a fool
you burrow roots deep in concrete, trouble
far from your fading consciousness. Though,
one day, when these walls crumble to rubble,
you will see that this city won't save you.

Loyal to an End

Steady as the sun, she arrives in the
morning and stays till my dark, weary eyes
embrace slumber. She bears my worst and sees
me through deep valleys. Her comforting lies
carry me through terrible night and then
her chilling presence chains me to indifference.
Her saccharine whisper has wearied my hurt
and surpassed suffering soul. Still she sends
me thoughtful gifts and beckons Hate's sharp
spurt.
She has seen my death and watched me wither,
for Grief is my most loyal lover.

Metaphysical Poetry?

I was a paper straw
She was an environmentally aware consumer
She appreciated what I was trying to do
But the execution was all wrong

She was the moon
I was an astronomer studying lunar phases
She was usually there for me
But when she wasn't, it was notable

Our relationship was a thinly-veiled, offensive
dog whistle
Posted on a boomer's Facebook account
No one was sure if we were serious
But they were worried nonetheless

Your touch was like a student procrastinating
And doing everything except their university
assignments
I knew it was bad for me
Yet I cherished every moment

And our good-bye was like a nationwide
lockdown
Caused by a contagious disease
It came out of nowhere
But still managed to ruin my year.

Celestial Beauty

She loves as the moon, dull and
too often absent. Her smile is the
stars, celestial beauty shimmering,
slowly dying. Her eyes are the
sunrise, disturbing thy saccharine
slumber. Her mind, the ocean,
shifting and turbulent, terrorised by
soulless tide, capricious and
sorrowful. Her heart, sentenced
to silence by the moon's day of
selfish disappearance.

Dusk's Promise

He carries evanescent beauty, Light
and Dark united in that perilous
matrimony at his beckon. The Night's
deathly chill become a warming repose.
Bright hue brought mellow, cooled by the thin,
calming stroke of his crass and frail fingers.
Speckled canvas hung low, suffocating
the light as his dim presence doth linger.
But Dusk's beauty alludes mere aesthetic
pleasure. His promise beyond the horizon
hidden. Whisp'ring a half-truth, chaotic,
fleeting, flashing in that awful union.
What evening brings, when that darkness
descend,
is promise that everything has its end.

My Abyss

Is anyone listening? I ask not
from fear of being forgotten, for
my mind is a meaningless blot
on the canvas of history. Nor
do I ask in lieu of self-assurance,
for my life story is speckled with
lonely nights and grand endurance
of reclusive cage and key. The pith
in my question is birthed of dread that I could
be heard deeply and clearly understood.